Living A Dream

By

N'wayitelo Bruce Chuma

Living A Dream

Living A Dream

Written by

N'wayitelo Bruce Chumo

Giyani,
Nkowa Nkowa
South Africa

Telephone: 073 2227 857

Email: nwayitelo.brucechuma@gmail.com

Published by

William Jenkins

4036 Pine Street
Burnaby BC V5G 1Z5
Canada
Email: williamhenryjenkins#gmail.com

Copyright N'wayitelo Bruce Chuma © 2018

ISBN Paperback: 978-1-928164-45-6
ISBN 10 Paperback: 1928164455
ISBN Electronic Book: 978-1-928164-46-3

All rights reserved. Without limiting the rights under copyright reserved above, no part of this publication may be reproduced, stored in or introduced into a retrieval system, or transmitted, in any form, or by any means (electronic, mechanical, photocopying, recording, or otherwise) without the prior written permission of both the copyright owner and the above publisher of this book.

Living A Dream

Living A Dream

Author

N'wayitelo Bruce Chuma was born in Mahlathi village, Giyani, South Africa. He did his primary at Vusizi Primary School then started his secondary at Giva Mahlathi High School. He later relocated to Nkowankowa where he matriculated at Hudson Ntsanwisi Senior Secondary

He has always been very ambitious towards his dreams, he is an open minded person and he is always pushing himself to the maximum limit. He enjoys motivating a lot and he believes he is capable of doing much more than his imagination.

His book is made up of different motivating essays which encourage the reader to never stop believing and always to work hard towards their ultimate dream.

Dedication

I dedicate this book to the youth of our present generation and generations to come.

Living A Dream

Contents

Author v
Dedication vi
Introduction 1
Success 2
    Creativity 2
    Purpose 2
    Boldness 3
    Sincerity 3
    Responsibility 3
    Availability 3
    Independence 3
    Gratefulness 4
    Confidence 4
Failure 5
    Lack of Purpose 5
    Fear 6
    Lack of Motivation 6
    Excuses 6
    Poor Choices 7
    Lack of Courage 7

Living A Dream

    Lack of Focus 8

    Overly Cautious 8

    Habits 8

Dreams 9

    Be Inspiring 9

    Be Passionate 10

    Have Integrity 10

    Avoid Bad Company 10

Be Realistic 11

    Hold Great Expectations 11

    Self-Strength 11

    Analyze Yourself 11

    Know Yourself 11

    Know What You Want 12

    Be Yourself 13

    Be a Visionary 14

    Overcome Doubts 15

    Plant your seed 16

    Mental Strength 16

Build your Faith 18

    Keep your Mind Clear 19

Living A Dream

Be helpful 19

Learn from your Mistakes 19

Mental Situations 20

Don't Be Comfortable 21

Time Is Limited 22

Time Management 24

Plan ahead 24

Eliminate distractions 24

Mistakes 25

Ignoring your priorities 25

Procrastinating 25

Losing Determination and Motivation 25

Second chances 26

Be a Winner 27

Improve Yourself Everyday 27

Be Committed 28

Be Patient 29

Be Approachable 30

Build a legacy 30

In Conclusion 31

Living A Dream

Introduction

I have a vision for a mission of teaching, helping, inspiring, motivating and entertaining each person who reads this book.

I want people to understand that dreams can be only dreams while you are still sleeping, but once you wake up you have the power to keep on living in the dream world or to make your dream a reality.

I hope to redirect the steps of those who are going in the wrong direction through this book.

I wish to give hope to those who are lost and motivation to those who think they cannot make their dreams a reality.

I believe that there are people who have dreams and goals, but who have no idea on how to achieve their goals and live their dreams. Some are struggling to continue with their projects because they are discouraged. I hope to restore their faith in themselves.

I truly believe that the power of emotions and feelings will comfort you. I believe that you will learn different things from the book and I hope you'll enjoy each topic.

In life, we will meet tribulations. We will meet many difficulties, but does it mean that we must give up? I don't believe so. You never fail until you stop trying.

Living A Dream

Success

There are many definitions of success. I believe that success is the ability to do whatever is necessary and possible in order to reach your destiny. It is the power to recreate your mind in a positive manner. Success involves designing opportunities in order to have a better tomorrow.

If you have dream, start acting on it, for you can never achieve your dream if you don't put your effort into it.

Dreams are not magically fulfilled. It takes dedication and a lot of effort to make your dreams come true. If you can decide to dedicate your life to winning, you can be the greatest winner the world has ever seen.

These are some of the factors that affect success:

Creativity

Creativity is the ability to design or develop something new. It is having the mentality of always trying new methods if the old ones did not function. For you to fulfill your dreams and goals, you must have some creativity within you and be able to come up with some fresh ideas. Become a designer of new strategies and come up with plans for your dreams.

Purpose

Purpose is the reason why a person does whatever he chooses to do. Living a life of purpose will help you to keep on holding onto your dream. A purposeful life will also keep you strong in times of tribulation.

If you know your purpose in life, it will always be the reminder of your dreams and provide the courage to keep you strong even when you feel like quitting.

Living A Dream

Boldness

Boldness is having the confidence that you'll achieve your plan no matter what the circumstances. It takes boldness for a dreamer to continue to chase his dream when others have given up.

Sincerity

Sincerity means being honest or meaning what you say. I believe you have to be honest with yourself and to be sure about the decisions you make, for they can forever transform your life negatively or positively.

Responsibility

Responsibility is accepting a duty to deal with or to take care of a situation. If anything goes wrong because of your action or inaction, you must take the blame. It's best to be responsible for every activity you do because the journey doesn't end on dreaming alone. It's your duty as a dreamer to make sure the dreams become reality.

Availability

Availability means being ready for anything. Your availability proves your willingness as to how far you are willing to go for that dream. If there's a show that you really love on TV, you'll always make sure that before that show starts you are already watching TV. The same method is applied in the area of dreams. Always be available for your dreams. Make time to work on your future regardless of your present condition.

Independence

Independence requires you to stand up for your own desires. To become someone special in the world you mustn't rely on others, but be able to create your own actions. Don't stand only with others because they might move and you might fall. Stop relying on other people. A person can change and might somehow disappoint you. That shouldn't be the end of your dreams. Continue to fight for your dreams to avoid disappointment.

Gratefulness

Gratefulness refers to appreciating something that someone has done for you. In showing your gratitude, you need to apply the statement that "actions speak louder than words". Your mouth might be saying one thing whereas your actions might say another thing. Show respect and honor those who helped you to get where you are. Be grateful for their efforts in your life. Show them gratitude. If you don't acknowledge their contribution, when you need their help again, they may not be so willing to assist you.

Confidence

Confidence is a state of being certain that you are truly capable of doing something. Even in tough times you mustn't stop, Faith starts from confidence. Before you believe in yourself, start by believing in your dreams. To believe in yourself, believe in your investment. Believe that you have what it takes. Never doubt your capabilities and believe that you're the best of the best.

Failure

According to the dictionary, failure is defined as the lack of success. However, I prefer to define failure as the power that makes a person unable to continue.

I gathered information about why many people become failures in life. I found out that many of the people who are not making it in life always make excuses. As my research went on, I found that many people gave up in life due to reasons such as:

- I didn't get enough time to chase my dream
- I didn't have resources to pursue my goals
- I didn't get the opportunity to express my ideas
- I was not a person for whom success was meant
- I wasn't wise enough to make it

However, I believe that a great deal of failure that the world is experiencing today is because of fear. People are afraid of failing. They do not want to do something because of the possibility of failure.

Nevertheless, I say that failing does not make a person a failure, but when you fear it, you are more likely to become a failure. To be successful in life you must not be afraid of failing, but be willing to try. If you fail, try again and again always modifying and improving your plan. When you keep on trying, the chances of getting it right are higher than when you do nothing.

These are some of the things that play a major role on failure:

Lack of Purpose

If you haven't yet discovered your purpose in life, it's too early for you to start on chasing after your dreams. You won't even have a direction to follow. Describe a reason why you should chase after a certain dream you're working on. Lack

Living A Dream

of purpose is lack of direction and without direction you'll always be lost. Be a purposeful dreamer and then you'll always chase what's right and useful. You'll never be misled or taken in the wrong direction. You'll always know what's right and how to achieve it.

Fear

Fear is the greatest enemy of success. It can be very dangerous. It can destroy your faith and hopes at the same time. Fear can make you feel useless and hopeless. It can make you fail to see the importance of dreams. A person with fear cannot do anything for they are full of "what if".

I believe that no one is perfect. If you are still fearing what others are going to say about you or if you fear rejection, you are likely to become a failure. For we all have fear, but we don't need to live ours when our desires are stronger than our fears.

Lack of Motivation

If you are motivated enough, it's easy for you to survive in the world of dreams. Dreams come with difficulties. If you don't have what it takes to hold on to your dreams no matter what challenges arise, then your dreams will be short-lived.

Success requires a lot of hard work. It is not simply dreaming that you will wake up tomorrow living your dream. You have to sweat for those dreams. You'll meet trials and tribulations along the journey, but if you are strongly motivated by your dreams then you can keep on holding them.

Excuses

Stop saying I can't, I couldn't or I'm too busy. Excuses are choices you make. If you choose not to complete your studies, don't claim that it's a matter of finances if truly you didn't want to continue studying.

What have you done to show that you really wished to move on with a specific project? Whenever you give excuses on why you are unable to chase after your dream, you are losing your investment in that dream bit by bit. In a while you'll find yourself having no dream because all the space for dreams will be filled with excuses.

It was once said that a negative attitude is like a flat tire in that you can't get anywhere with it. I believe that even when a shop can sell the most amazing stock that no other shop can sell, if the behavior of the shop keeper or the cashier is negative towards the customers, no one will want to buy at that shop.

If your attitude is negative, it will also affect your dreams because having a negative attitude results in negative behavior that looks as though you are unable to control yourself. When you can't control yourself, you'll be chasing people who initially wanted to invest in that dream of yours.

Poor Choices

Mostly poor choices are made by people who are under a certain influence. It can be an influence of friends, drugs or even alcohol, but I assure you that a poor choice can cause a huge damage to your future. If you are still unable to make right choices regarding your destiny, then you are likely to reach a wrong destination at the end. I believe that decision making is a skill which all dreamers must acquire in order to make beneficial choices in life.

Lack of Courage

If you don't have enough courage, you'll always give up when people tell you it is impossible to achieve that dream.

Living A Dream

Be strong and courageous. The word "impossible" itself says "I'm possible". It's true that others weren't able to complete that investment, but you were born to break that cycle.

Lack of Focus

The strength of our focus determines the level of our achievements. How focused you are on your studies determines your result. The same thing is true for the world of your future. When you can't concentrate on the main priority or the main goal, your mind is all over the place. Then you cannot survive in the world of dreams. Make your dreams a main focus. Live as though it's your only reason for living.

Overly Cautious

A great man once said "the higher you climb the harder you fall and the more you fall the faster you get stronger to climb again". In greater risks there are greater rewards. If you are afraid to take a risk for your dreams, then you don't belong in the world of dreams.

Habits

Everyone has their way of doing things. How we do things determines the outcome. If you decide to be a leader and still act like a staff member, do you think the staff will take you seriously? I don't think so. How you conduct your life proves how serious you are towards your goal. It's time to stop blaming others and take responsibility for your actions; it's time to change your tomorrow. Destroy your older habits and start creating a better future for yourself.

Living A Dream

Dreams

A dream is a picture of yourself that you created in your mind for the future; it is how you see yourself in the future. I believe that dreams can be very powerful. How you see yourself in future will determine you will actually live. Examine yourself. What do you wish to have? How do you wish to live? Do you have a dream? Do you wish to have something tomorrow?

Dreams don't come overnight. You have to sweat for them. I believe that everything that was invented in this world started from dreams. Even those who invented the smart phones first pictured them in their mind before starting to build them practically. They met challenges along the journey. They failed from time to time in the process, but that didn't stop them from pursuing their dream. They tried again and again until they made it.

If you have a dream today, on your way to fulfill it you'll sometimes meet hardships and disappointment. Don't let them end your journey. You can still carry on. You can still run that race that shows you are meant for greatness.

Dreams are mostly based on what's influencing you in the moment. Everyone who has a dream of becoming a medical doctor knows what a medical doctor is.

These are some of the things that each dreamer must have in order to succeed in the world of dreams:

Be Inspiring

As a dreamer, for you to survive in this world of dreams, let your dreams be inspiring. Dream of something new, something that doesn't exist now. Let people be inspired by your dreams. Dream something mind blowing, something that will amaze everyone.

Living A Dream

Be Passionate

It is best for you to be passionate about whatever dream you pursue. If you are not passionate enough, you'll sometimes think you are no longer doing the right thing because you don't love the dream that you are chasing. When you are passionate about something, you are truly sure about it. Even if your actions don't prove out, people will notice how serous you are.

Have Integrity

Being a person with great integrity can attract investors in your dreams. Although you may lack motivation, people will want to associate with you because of the integrity you'll be showing. At your lowest moments, these people will lift you up because of the respect you'll be showing them. That can have a positive effect on your dreams.

Avoid Bad Company

Birds of a feather flock together. For you to make it in life you must be careful of the company you keep. Every person whose company you keep influences you to become like them. You cannot be different from those with whom you closely associate. If you keep bad company you must make sure you're more effective in changing their lives rather them being more effective in changing yours. Be aware that bad company will affect your dreams and visions when you let them influence you.

Be Realistic

Hold Great Expectations

Expectation is the courage to look forward to a better future even though there might be no indication to justify that you can actually achieve your dreams. A person with expectations will always do things that are purposeful. If expect to do something concerning your dreams, you'll do it with high confidence because what you have in mind is far better than the reality.

Self-Strength

There are none as powerful as those who rely on their strength and potential. A person who failed in life probably mistakenly misunderstood the word impossible. There's nothing impossible in this world. What is possible is based on your faith; how you believe in your dreams. You should not stop fighting for that dream because it is possible.

Analyze Yourself

People, especially the youth, often avoid this process. They don't have this self-session and in most cases they end up forgetting about their true self. They forget their goal and the reasons they were created. They end up following a meaningless life style. I say that having a serious talk with yourself is the greatest step one can take, for it analyzes your true self and helps you discover why you are the way you are today. It also helps you to understand what you can do to be what you wish to be.

Know Yourself

People are unsure of who they are in life. They forget their dreams and goals. They do things not because they want to do those things but because others are doing those things. They forget what they want and chase what others want and end up with what they don't really need.

A king may try to rule the way a king from another country did. He may end up destroying his nation because he implemented the right methods on the wrong congregation.

You should know yourself and what you want. Knowing your true self is the process which anyone who wishes to be great in life must go through. The process helps us to know our strengths and our weaknesses. To be the best you can be, you must first find where your potential lies. Be sure of every decision you make. See if you're really interested in whatever you want to do.

Each decision you take today can determine your future. Generate new ideas today; make new dreams; set new goals; set new timelines. Do new things that will reveal your true self.

Consider a soccer match where you're playing against a very well-known rival team. Do you think you can ever defeat them without knowing their strategies and weaknesses? You don't need to know their secret for winning a match. Discover their weaknesses and then use that to your advantage.

The same thing applies in the world of dreams. Before you can start chasing your dreams, you must first be sure about yourself. Be sure about your dreams; then you'll achieve more than you can imagine.

Know What You Want

Knowing what you want in life can also be helpful because it can make you stay focused. It can make you know the abilities that you can use to your advantage. If you have

Living A Dream

already figured out what you want to do with your life, then start striving to make your dreams a reality.

No matter how hard it may seem to be holding on to your dreams, don't give up what you want or you will end up with what you don't want. Try not to choose a certain lifestyle because of the environment you are living in at the moment. Be yourself. Make sure you're following your own goals. That way you know your earlier lifestyle won't be a disgrace to you in future years.

In order for you to make it in this world, you must be willing and determined. You must be ready to live with all the consequences and be able to really strive for greatness.

To achieve you must be prepared to meet all the requirements and to obey each of them.

You must be patient and pay careful attention to detail.

Always remember why you are chasing that dream so that you will stay on the right track.

Don't be discouraged by the negativity of other people.

Stay focused on your goals and concentrate on them.

Be Yourself

What does it mean to be yourself? Being yourself is a state of knowing your inner self, knowing what does and what doesn't make you happy. It's being able to pursue your dreams no matter the challenges. I know that people may not always appreciate you. They might sometimes discourage you, but the only way to achieve a satisfying dream is to stay true to yourself.

Don't quit because others failed, but break that cycle of failure. Even those who are close to you might sometimes not agree with what you have in heart, but even when no one is supportive of the fact that what you doing makes you

Living A Dream

happy, continue because you don't need to entertain others to make it. You just have to do what's right.

People might say that you are chasing after fantasy or you're trying to do the impossible, but you don't have to listen to these comments because in most cases those who are discouraging you are those who tried and failed. They convinced themselves that it's impossible so they try to convince you that such greatness is impossible.

If to achieve something were impossible then even to dream about it would also have been impossible. An eagle that flies very high in the sky does so not because it's more special than other birds. It does so because an eagle can see its potential and believes in its abilities.

Even you as a dreamer can believe in yourself and trust in your potential. Let your eyes be sharp like those of eagles so you can predict the future by today's conditions.

Even though you may be facing challenges from all four corners of the earth, the troubles are not meant to keep you down, but to help you discover yourself and your purpose in this land of the living.

If you're not doing something that makes you smile, something that makes you proud and happy, then perhaps it is time for a new plan.

Be a Visionary

A vision is an ideal or goal towards which one aspires. What are your visions? What goals do you have? How many years will it take you to achieve them? Dreams occur when you sleep. When you wake up the power becomes in your hands.

The ability of making it in life starts from having a vision. Do you have a vision of your own? Write it down for you might forget your purpose in life. Dream huge, aim high and accomplish more.

Living A Dream

To become the greatest in the world you must be able to look into the future, to aim for tomorrow before it arrives. Let your vision make a way for you; let your vision become your target.

Someone said that the wealthiest place you can ever find in the planet is the graveyard because there you'll find visions that were never acted upon, dreams that were never lived, goals that were never achieved.

Now is your moment to act upon your vision, to live those dreams, to reach that goal; for if you do not live your dreams, you are going to work for others and help them live theirs.

Overcome Doubts

People start discouraging themselves in life because of doubts. Once you start doubting yourself then you are traveling in a path that will automatically lead you to nowhere. Of course, everyone has doubts in life. Even the most successful people once had their doubts in their own project. What made them who they are today is the fact that they were able to overcome their doubts.

Do not let doubts bring you down. Always be inspired to be more, to do more. Be willing to achieve higher than your expectations, to climb higher than the limitations. Forget about the side effects that the kind of career you want have, but concentrate on what is positive about it.

When people start doubting their abilities, start doubting their own strength, it may be because of some senseless doubt such as...

- What if I fail and disappoint myself?
- What if I don't make it?
- What if I'm not good enough?
- What if I don't have what it takes?

Living A Dream

- What if I'm not what they are looking for?
- What makes me think I can do it?

To win in life you must overcome the doubts, because doubts make you achieve less than your full potential. It doesn't matter what kind of negative results and disappointments you might be having. Failing is always temporary in life. What matters is how you overcome doubts and overwhelm them with the strength of a positive mind.

Plant your seed

When a farmer plants a seed in his farm, the seed doesn't grow immediately after the planting. It undergoes some process and it takes long enough for the seed to germinate before a new plant can be produced. When the farmer is planting that seed he doesn't know which one will not grow and which one will grow in that soil, but he believes that all his seeds together will produce a valued product eventually.

The same process must be applied in the human nature. When you have a dream you must plant that seed in your heart. You'll face a lot of challenges after planting that dream. Just as a seed needs to be germinated before becoming a plant, you must overcome hardships before you reach your dreams.

Your difficulties may be financial, time management, friends or community. It doesn't matter, but note that the process is a must. Whether you like it or not you have to undergo that process of overcoming the difficulties.

Mental Strength

One day when I was going home from school, I passed through a shop. The shop owner looked very tired and I said to him "rough day it must have been". The man said to me "I'm no longer sure whether I'm only tired or overstressed or

Living A Dream

both". I felt pain in my heart looking at him, realizing that he is willing to do anything to put food on his table and noticing how hard it could be for him to dedicate his life to his business and not have many customers.

Your true strength lies in your mind. It doesn't matter what difficulties you are going through. If you can tell yourself that you'll never fail nor fall, it is not going to happen.

Life is based on choices. The choices you make today will affect not only your today, but also the rest of your future. You are capable to do more than your imagination describes. If you can apply the mental strength and stop caring about the situation, you'll do far better than what you think is your limit.

We see the mental strength mostly during sports. Check whenever someone is racing and they are about to reach the finishing line, you'll realize that suddenly they'll have an abnormal strength that will enable them to run as if they've just started the race.

Build your Faith

My mentor and motivator once said "a brain is like a circuit switch. Once you believe in something you actually take that feeling into consideration".

Let's say you had a massive accident and you were in a coma for the past two years. Then you wake up with a memory loss and you are told you used to be a professional soccer player and they want you back at the field when you are healthy. Do you think you would do things the way you're doing presently? No, you'll hold yourself differently. You'll conduct yourself in a different manner than when you say I wish or hope to be a professional soccer player.

To be the greatest winner of all time, start by believing in yourself. Believe that you have what it takes. Believe that you're someone unique, someone on a mission, and someone with a vision. Believe that you're someone special. Believe that you are that person you're always dreaming of becoming.

When you're building your faith you must understand that not everyone you're running with will finish the race; not everyone you're moving with is going the same direction. Therefore, in order to reach your destination you have to know some of the following:

- In all the advice you get you must consult before acting upon it because it may lead to distractions.
- Never lose hope. Even when the situation becomes even more impossible, believe that it is possible.
- Sometimes you might not get the kind of information you're looking for and some may refuse to help you, but have extreme faith in yourself.

Living A Dream

- Have self-control and be responsible for all your actions.
- Don't set timelines for your dreams because missing a particular step can make you lose faith and focus.
- Let all your mistakes become your lessons and motivation.

These are some of the things that can help you to have a greater faith:

Keep your Mind Clear

As long you're still breathing, you'll meet some problems and discouragements along the road. Some will be jealous of you. Whenever they try to pull you down, your mind must be focusing on your dreams and nothing else.

For those who aren't able to achieve what you are attempting, it will always be an impossible goal to achieve. They will try hard to make you believe that in the name of protecting you from failure, but you'll never fail until you try and you never get up until you fall.

Be helpful

I encourage you to start taking part in small projects for self-motivation. Start with small achievements. Be a helper. Let people start praising the good things you have done for them for that can have a great impact on self-motivation and it will start the fire of "I can do it" inside of you.

Learn from your Mistakes

Mistakes you once made often come back to haunt your future. There are things in life that are unable to be changed, but we can learn to adjust and move on with life. Parental mistakes are not our fault. The fact that you can't go forward

Living A Dream

with your studies because your parents are not able to provide financial support isn't your fault, but when you see that they are doing whatever they can for you to have a better tomorrow and you ignore the opportunity, then it is your fault.

You don't build your dreams because of certain conditions, but because it is your goal to make your dreams a reality. It was once said that if you are not busy building your dreams while time is still in your side, you'll help others complete their goals.

Worrying about what may have occurred in your past is a total waste of time and energy. It is just the thing to make you feel that you can't do it. Challenges and differences are faced by everyone, but we make a choice whether to stay down and be victimized by our past or to stand up and overcome those limitations to reach success in its full potential.

Mental Situations

Some of the enemies we fight in life are the enemies we embrace within us. The greatest enemy that can make you to fail in life is yourself. Your belief can be a powerful weapon used for or against your victory.

Once I was passing by a road while I was traveling to school and I saw something very interesting. There was a donkey that seemed to be just like other donkeys, but there was something special about it. As I was passing by, all the other donkeys started running, but this one donkey didn't run. I stopped, wondering why this donkey did not run while others ran away.

I took a good look at that donkey and I saw something like a rubber on its legs. I asked the owner of the donkey "Sir, why do all the other donkeys run away and that one does not even bother to move"? The owner told me that the rubber-like thing that I saw is what prevents that donkey from moving. He said that he used that rubber-like rope to tie the donkey since it was born and when the donkey is bound by that rope it believes it cannot move no matter how hard it tries.

Then I thought to myself that many people are like this donkey. It is not that we cannot achieve our dreams and goals, but rather, like that donkey, we think we cannot achieve them because that's what we have convinced ourselves. Today people are trying but not getting success and are quitting on their dreams because like that donkey they think they cannot do it.

For you to make it in life, for you to be a success in life, change your mentality. Stop being bound by things that are weak. Get over that feeling that says it's impossible and believe that you're going to make it possible.

Don't Be Comfortable

People start coping with situations and they begin to forget their dreams. You will never reach your goals when you are still waiting for the dream to say come catch me. Your goals will never wait for you. You have to run towards them for you to catch them.

You will sometimes think that you're waiting for the right moment, for the right opportunity, for the right timing, but unless you decide to stand up, to create your own opportunities, you will look for the opportunity that will never come.

Strive to achieve better things than what you have already achieved. Wherever you are, stand up and look forward. You'll always see further. To achieve any greatness you want in life, you have to pay the price for it.

Living A Dream

Start adopting a proper mindset so your vision will become your direction. Do not allow yourself to be satisfied, for satisfaction can lead to comfort and comfort leads to distractions. When you stay in your comfort zone, you will never be able to make your dreams a living reality.

Time Is Limited

Each day everyone is given the same amount of time. Whatever time you fail to invest wisely is recorded as a loss for that day. Spend your time wisely; invest in something beneficial. Remember, time lost can never be regained. Make the most of today's time while you're still able to do so.

My mentor once that "you will never realize the value of the opportunity you're having until you've lost it". He said as well "to realize the value of one year, ask the student who just failed a grade; to realize the value of one month, ask a mother who just gave birth to a premature baby; to realize the value of one week, ask the editor of a weekly newspaper; to realize the value of one day, ask a person who missed an interview; to realize the value of one hour ask a person who just missed a train; to realize the value of one second ask a person who nearly had an accident". Time waits for no man. Do everything necessary make every second count.

Whatever you're doing, however you're spending your time, will determine how successful you'll be in the future.

How much time do you invest in your dreams? How much time do you spend trying to live your dreams, to make your goals a reality? What are you doing to prepare your future? In the past few days, what new skills or knowledge have you acquired? What investment you have made in yourself?

Today, millions of people are busy doing nothing; they are busy sleeping, busy socializing or even busy watching

Living A Dream

television. People are destroying their own dreams because of the hours they spend watching others living their dreams.

The creator of video games that you spend thousands of hours playing is living his dreams; the question is when are you living yours?

Start reserving your energy for your highest and best use. Greater and mighty people have had exactly the same amount of time as everyone else. However, they invested their time in their dreams. They made an effort in what they really believe and wanted to achieve.

No matter how long it may take, don't stop running towards your dreams. You can never fail until you stop moving. Don't postpone your dreams.

Time Management

For you to make it in this world of dreams you must have time management. If you don't manage your time, your dreams will be disorganized. You won't do things according to a plan because you lose track of time, mix up your activities, and confuse yourself.

Here are some of the things you should do to manage your time in the right way:

Plan ahead

As a person with a vision you must able to see the future by looking at present conditions, so it is best for you to plan ahead. Let your plans be ones that guarantee you a better tomorrow and a future you cannot regret.

Eliminate distractions

When you decide to take an unessential break to check on Twitter, it is the first step towards losing your focus. The more you check Whatsapp, the more your concentration is reduced. When you don't spend time investing in your future, you lessen the chance of obtaining a better future.

A person without concentration is always distracted. if you're always distracted then it's time to create a schedule that's suitable for you. Without concentration you lose your dream and that's nor useful.

Mistakes

We all sometimes do make mistakes. To learn from your mistakes is not mandatory, but rather a choice. The following are some of the mistakes we make:

Ignoring your priorities

When you fail to keep to your first priority you are likely to become a failure in life. Create a priority list that will help you focus on what's important. It will also tell what to do at a certain moment.

Procrastinating

You are procrastinating when you are not doing what you're supposed to do at that certain time, putting off indefinitely what you should do today. Procrastination occurs in the life of people who haven't developed their time management skills.

Losing Determination and Motivation

One writer said that "determination is the ability to achieve a goal no matter hard or difficult it is to achieve". There is nothing a determined and motivated person can fail to achieve. When you start by believing in yourself and focus on your goals, there is no dream you can fail to accomplish.

Stand up and start fighting towards your dreams no matter how slim the chance of winning may seem. You can make it. Start by doing whatever you can today. Start acting with that feeling that says you can do it because you actually can.

Living A Dream

Second chances

Many people are not worried about doing things correctly on the first opportunity, but instead they say they'll do it on the second chance.

Be careful of second chances; appreciate the fact that you have a chance now so why wait for another chance if you have a chance to improve now. Life is not like a soccer match. There are no rematches or replays. Opportunity comes once in a lifetime and if you miss your opportunity, you'll have to create another one for yourself.

Stop telling yourself "I'll do it correctly later". Do it correctly now. Why wait for later when the time is now? It's not a time to make mistakes, but time to get it right on the first try. You don't know that this may be your first and only opportunity.

Be a Winner

I believe that winning is the matter of choice. In life we are all given the opportunity whether to make it or to quit and become a failure. You choose to give up; you choose to stop dreaming. You can end your future before it's even started.

It's not too late. Today you can start winning; you can still make it in life. It doesn't matter how many opportunities you have wasted, you can still get another chance, perhaps not as good a chance as the one you rejected, but still a chance to advance. You can still dream your own dreams. You can still achieve more and you can still win big.

It is never too late. As long you're still breathing, you can still make your move, you can still play your part in your project. The common regret most people have is how they were not able to achieve their vision. It is now your time to up your game, to make your own legacy.

As long as the human brain is involved, there is nothing impossible. You can reach your destiny, you can discover that cure, and you can stop that cycle. Start today and achieve better than expected.

Improve Yourself Everyday

One way of defeating failure in life is by improving yourself every day. Yes, you might not always get it correct, but that does not mean you should throw in the towel. You can still find hope in any situation.

Always review the mistakes you make and look for a way of preventing them. If there seems to be no way out, try looking for assistance from those who have had the same difficulty. Their help can really improve the way you handle the matter.

Try to do more today than you did yesterday. Try to do better than last time. Whenever you continue moving at the same pace, whenever you are achieving at the same level, you are not improving. If you always practice things that you have already mastered, then you are not improving but rehearsing what you already know. Become original, be new; start brainstorming new ideas, for you are destined for greatness.

Forget what happened to you yesterday for you can never change history and all that has happened in it. You can do something today that can change your future for better.

Many people are failing in whatever they are trying to do today not because they don't possess the required potential, but because they are trying to perfect the dreams that have been designed by others. I believe that chasing after fantasy is trying to redesign the ideas that were originally not yours. Dreams are not about the wrongs and mistakes you may have made. As long as you're still breathing there's actually a chance for you to make it right.

Be Committed

Commitment is the power to focus no matter what happens. It is the courage to keep on believing regardless of the situation. Commitment is being prepared to give all your time, your attention and your heart to whatever you are planning to do.

Without commitment you'll always find it difficult to achieve each goal you plan on achieving. I believe that you'll always get what you are committed to. You can achieve either the desired result or a meaningless excuse as to why you failed.

Commitment is an act of motion. It's not about how much you say or try to prove how committed you are, but it's your result that makes noise about your commitment. The kind of result that you'll get from your project will be determined by the investment you make.

Living A Dream

The result you get in your studies is determined by how committed you are when it's time to do your school work.

Be committed to greatness. The results that you can produce will be determined by the level of your commitment in that production. Commitment is the only thing that keeps a person motivated when others are quitting and losing their dreams. Your commitment will give you the strength to hold on.

Be Patient

Patience is the courage to hold on your dreams, to stay strong, to stay focused and to always move in the right direction. The road to achieve greater things is seldom easy. As you push forward the more difficult it becomes. If you have patience, you'll never give up on your dreams, but keep on moving to get what you wish to accomplish.

Be patient enough to know that even if it may rain for years, one day the rain will stop. If it doesn't stop, you'll have to find a way through that rain to make your dream a reality.

A patient person knows that things won't always go according to the plans and purposes, but even in that hardest situation where there are millions of reasons to give up, he'll always find one reason to keep on, to keep having faith and to work until he reaches his goals.

Success is not about how fast you can reach your dreams, but it's based on how far are you willing to go to reach those dreams. Someone said "success is sweet and sweeter if long delayed and if you went through many struggles, pains and defeats".

I believe that the journey of a thousand miles begins with the first step. It's not about how far or how long it can take you to finish the race. What's important is that at the end, you'll finish the race.

Living A Dream

Be Approachable

One way to get people's support is to be approachable, For you to be supported by the community or people around you, you must have a good attitude, be caring, be friendly, show generosity, and make those people look up to you.

People trust what they know. When you make them feel comfortable around you, they will have more confidence in your inventions and they will help you take your dream to the next level.

The more people are comfortable around you the more you win, When someone believes in your dreams, they will want to make sure that your dreams become a reality. So, even when you might be facing financial difficulties those people who you have inspired by the way you do things will want to invest in those dreams.

Build a legacy

The things we are doing eventually build our legacies. The actions we are taking and how we live our lives represent how we are going to be remembered. You should do something that you are proud of while you can.

Even when you build a toilet if that's the kind of legacy you want to leave it's fine because dreaming doesn't mean the dream should be huge or mind blowing but the dream must be interesting to someone who is dreaming it. Let your legacy describe your achievement. Leave a mark on this planet.

In Conclusion

You are capable of doing more than you imagine. You can do more by using your abilities. Stand up for your dream. Defeat the enemy in your mind that says you can't do it, for you are capable of doing things that are greater than you imagine. Success and failure lie between I can and I can't. Everything is possible. It is your mind that makes something seem to be impossible. You can win. You can achieve what you want because it is possible.

You are on this planet for a greater purpose. Your life is the light in the world. Instead of crying and mourning, it's time to shine those ideas, those inventions. Every one of us is carrying something greater inside. It's just a matter of living those dreams. You can be whatever you want to be if you can make a decision today, a decision to strive for your greatness, to overcome fear and chase after what you really want.

Don't let anyone intimidate you; don't let them decide your fate. You were born for greatness. You were not created to suffer, but you are destined for greater purposes.

The current conditions do not determine your future. No matter what you are facing today, what is happening in your life, look at the situation positively. Don't try to blame others or your creator, but believe that you can make a change. Believe that you are the solution to difficulties and you'll be successful.

www.ingramcontent.com/pod-product-compliance
Lightning Source LLC
Chambersburg PA
CBHW061006050426

42453CB00009B/1286